When Lightning Strikes
(Nikola's Dove)

Nikola Tesla, 1890

When Lightning Strikes
(Nikola's Dove)

poems by
Tracy Ross

SHANTI ARTS PUBLISHING
BRUNSWICK, MAINE

When Lightning Strikes
(Nikola's Dove)

Copyright © 2023 Tracy Ross

All Rights Reserved
No part of this document may be reproduced or transmitted in any form or by any means without prior written permission of the publisher, except in the case of brief quotations embodied in critical reviews.

Published by Shanti Arts Publishing

Designed by Shanti Arts Designs

Shanti Arts LLC
193 Hillside Road
Brunswick, Maine 04011
shantiarts.com

This activity was made possible by an Artist Grant provided by the Prairie Lakes Regional Arts Council from funds provided by the McKnight Foundation.

Printed in the United States of America

ISBN: 978-1-956056-98-3

Library of Congress Control Number: 2023942492

*For my brother, Eric,
and all the generations that have paved the way.*

Contents

Energy for All	10
Someone Is Calling	11
What Hath God Wrought!	12
Wires, Wires Everywhere (Steps in the Wrong Direction)	13
Progeny Names and Morse Code (False Equivalencies)	14
Communication Graffiti	15
Tethered by Wires, Separated by Distance (A Father's Disconnect)	16
The Children Will Abide	17
The Measure of a Man and Child	18
New Innocence, Visions	20
Heaven Speaks for the Gentlefolk	22
Angels of Disconnect, Fast Forward	24
Please Listen	25
A Young Man Holds the Light	26
Through the Window	28
Silver Serpents of Entropy	29
Body Resistance	30
I Get the Destination—Coffee for One	32
Old Earth Decay, New Earth Visions	34
Normal in the Chaos	36
What Is Beneath the Disguise	38
Look Back in Anger	40
The Cost of Captured Lightning	41
Magnetism and the Lonely Heart	42
Edison in Kansas	43
A Brutal Education in America	44
The War of the Currents	46
Cutting the Cords	48
Signs	51
Flying Through the Years	52

Know the Moment	53
Behold a Pale Horse	56
The War of the Currents Is Won	60
Access and the Global Brass Ring	63
The Reigns and Purse Strings	65
The Lightning in Ely, Minnesota	67
Energy's Grail	70
The Heart Will Follow	72
Nature's Light at the End of the Road	74
The Machinery at the Bottom of the Sea	77
Battles with the Virtual World	79
The Great White Elephant	81
Keeping the Ghost Close	84
Kind Gestures	86
My Brother's Care	88
After Wardenclyffe	90
Nervous Breakdowns	92
We Are Not Who We Seem to Be	94
Don't Mind the Clock	95
Long Day's Journey into Light	96
The Oath of the Gentlefolk	98
Hope Is Watching the Weather	100
Nikola's Dove	102
Notes	105
About the Author	107

Nikola's Dove

Energy for All

I am a small, eight-year-old girl,
sitting on the porch in the rain.
I watch as a flag pole in the distance
gets struck by lightning.
There is no flag on the pole,
but its steel ropes and cords
make sounds in the wind—
clank, clank, clank!
The sky turns dark, opening with storms,
a Jacob's ladder forming between the clouds and the ground,
with the sunlight breaking through in ripples.
I look up, seeing telephone wires
stretching from pole to pole,
blocking my vision of the clear blue.
Birds come and sit momentarily on the wires,
turning their heads to hear the sounds below.

There are no more trees,
there is no more grass,
just cars, the Motor City building cars...
And when the morning comes,
the sky will be full of smoke and brilliant colors
produced from the pollution of the factories.
It will be beautiful—
as surreal as a Salvador Dali dream.
The barren morning of our possibility.

Someone Is Calling

The lightning is calling.
The phone wires are calling.
The storms are calling.
The sky is so big when the lightning strikes,
it calls my name,
the angels knowing full well
I will remember the storms of 1977
like they were yesterday's roses,
my brain, the collective consciousness—
Pavlov's dog responding to some distant bell
and pulling me forward
into some Utopian future of free energy for all.

Watch the lightning strike,
wait like a soldier of tomorrow—
the sky reflected in the child's eyes,
an electric heaven promising freedom.

Clank–clank–clank!
The future is calling.

Clank–clank–clank!
Nature responds in kind.

What Hath God Wrought!

In 1840, Samuel Morse patented his electromagnetic telegraph.
On the rainy day of May 24, 1844, in Washington, D.C.,
Annie Ellsworth, a lovely lady and acquaintance of Morse,
handed Samuel the message she had chosen to be the first wired script.
It exclaimed, "What hath God wrought!" (1)

Still in Washington's Supreme Court offices,
Samuel tapped out the words on the key to his friend,
Alfred Vail, in Baltimore.
Alfred mirrored back the same four words
as confirmation that Morse's machine had worked:
"What hath God wrought!" (2)

    Station to station—confirmations.

Wires, Wires Everywhere
(Steps in the Wrong Direction)

How do you eliminate the distance
created by wires and cables,
industriously put down under land and sea
by hard physical labor?

How do you reverse the stripping of the natural world
for the benefit of our conversation?

   Station to station—confirmations.

Say goodbye to the old world
of saying hello through our hard copy messages,
carried on the backs of men and horses.
Say goodbye via telegraph
and watch the continents shift at your demand.

   "What hath God wrought...?"

We returned the favor with our tangled web,
our attempt to connect our hearts with wire.
The copper that made the wire
made those in the tower very rich indeed.

Progeny Names and Morse Code
(False Equivalencies)

As a young child, Thomas Edison so loved the telegraph
he even worked along the railroad system,
learning all he could of Samuel's machine. (3)
On Christmas Eve of 1871,
Thomas married sixteen-year-old Mary Stillwell.
The young couple had three children.
When the first, Marion Estelle, was born in 1873,
Edison chose to nickname her *Dot*.
When the second, Thomas Alva Edison Jr., was born in 1876,
Edison chose to nickname him *Dash*.
The third child, born in 1878,
was given the name William Leslie.
He graduated from Yale's Sheffield Scientific School in 1900. (4)

You are like a son to me. You are like a daughter to me. Are you a child? Are you a thing? Take these ciphers from me, and carry them with you as placeholders of the soul. You are an extension of my ego, so you cannot possess my unconditional love. You are an extension where the symbols go, so you cannot take from me what I forever own. You are mine. You are just like me and will go forth in your obedience. Don't disappoint me because you know better.

Communication Graffiti

As a child, I collected rain water in glass jars.
My mother once told me
that it was softer and healthier than water from the tap—
so soft you could wash your hair with it,
so fresh you could drink it from the sky.
This was all I knew,
this and the sound the thunder made after the lightning,
my mind counting the seconds that passed between the two
to measure the proximity of the storm in miles.
I stayed quiet and let my eyes take in the information...
the sky resembling the bluish-gray crayon
in my Crayola box of 64 colors.

Soon, like the sky, all incoming information—
sights, sounds, smells, the strokes of the wind on my small face,
came to me in colors of bluish-gray crayon.
Shades of bluish-gray,
the color of metal and steel and iron.
The color of my childhood.
The color of tomorrow.

I used a piece of chalk and wrote to Dot and Dash,
waving at them from 1973,
thinking they would see me below from the sky above.
I inscribed their names on the sidewalk in Morse code.
Over and over, dot and dash, dot and dash,
dot and dash, dot and dash,
dot and dash, dot and dash...
until I got tired
and the rain
finally washed
the chalk away.

Tethered by Wires, Separated by Distance (A Father's Disconnect)

Samuel Morse's machine
was designed to communicate through wires
when humans briefly held down the key,
producing a quick click designating a *dot*,
or when the key was held down slightly longer,
producing a *dash*. (5)
Thomas Edison Sr. used to send his daughter,
Marion Estelle,
out often to buy him his cigars.
Thomas Sr. sent his son, Thomas Alva,
to boarding schools
in Concord, New Hampshire
and Staten Island, New York.

Dot goes out to purchase cigars for her father.
Dash goes to study far away in isolated rooms.

Dot wears pretty dresses with ribbons tied in her hair.
Dash wears his shoes polished and his pants long.
William Leslie, just called William,
tries to succeed as a scientist. (6)

The Children Will Abide

More than anyone,
I relate to Edison's children.
Born of a new age and having few choices,
they saw the writing on the wall.
They saw their father's demagoguery
and human error change the world.
For better or worse,
they were the next generation
to carry the torch,
the fire burning in their hearts
and setting the rivers on fire.
As their father attempted dominion,
they realized only fools
inherit the kingdom.
They had no choice
but to play in the chaos
and decay.

The Measure of a Man and Child

Thomas Edison asked his son Dash
to change his name after the young man
sold the use of the family last name
to market bogus medicines and inventions.
For a while, Thomas Alva did this,
becoming known by some as Thomas *Willard*.
Young Thomas Willard even tried his hand
at mushroom farming,
although it ultimately failed.
Dot and Dash Edison were befriended
by many of their father's acquaintances.
Henry Ford used to give them both automobiles as gifts,
so much so that they could never drive all of them
but kept them in storage garages.

In 1910, on the gray afternoon of October 2,
the *New York Times Magazine* asked Thomas Edison Sr. his
thoughts and he replied:

Nature is what we know.
We do not know the gods of religions,
and nature is not kind, or merciful,
or *loving* . . .
If God made me . . . the fabled God of the
three qualities of which I spoke:
mercy, kindness, love—
He also made the fish
I catch and eat.
And where do His mercy,
kindness, and love for that fish come in?
No. Nature made us.

Nature did it all.
Not the gods of the religions. (7)

To deny the creator is to replace him with yourself, hence,
there ceases to be a ceiling on Prometheus's dream.
I am not a creature, I am a man of free will and decision.
So get out of my way and do as you are told.
Respect my position as a replacement
for your farthest wishes and know
that all you aspire toward must be reduced
to what I can use it for.
For we are not playthings of Gods,
we are ringmasters of a great fate,
a fate made of perpetual motion
and aimless notions.

New Innocence, Visions

From a very young child, Nikola Tesla loved nature.
With innocent curiosity,
he keenly watched birds and their flight.
His childlike naivety of trying to use an open umbrella
to propel him in flight ended in being ill with a bad cold.
Nikola was sick much as a child, several times rather seriously.
Years later, the young boy spent much time
on the mountain watching lightning strike during storms.
Nikola's young years,
especially after the death of his older brother,
were mostly friendless.
He soon found he lacked a connection with others,
yet, he needed them just the same. (8)

Tesla's brother died in a horse-riding accident.
The memories get lost somehow.
Nothing remains clear through the passage of time.
The first of many motion picture shows—
a man riding a horse in slow motion—
Eadweard Muybridge, 1878.
Over and over.
Imprinted on the brain as if on celluloid—
the horse gallops and caries us through our motions—
the precipice of our fate always approaching
falling forward but being caught
by the legs
carrying weight
in descent
against gravity.

Is destiny this fragile?
Am I at fault for being so human
as to be a witness to death
and being able to do nothing?
I am sorry, my brother. I am so sorry . . .

Heaven Speaks for the Gentlefolk

Nikola Tesla, with his only real close friends
being his two sisters and his mother,
confessed that his inclinations at inventing
were inherited from his mother.

Nikola greatly admired women.
Yet, often,
the painful disconnect was overwhelming.

Across from Nikola's New York shop,
he greatly enjoyed bringing the pigeons
sustenance during the afternoons.
If he happened to be kept up
in his lab with an invention,
he would pay the messenger boy
to feed them so they'd be fed that day.
The windows in his New York lab
were always kept open so that the birds
could perch on the machinery if needed
for a respite from their daily flights.

As Nikola worked tirelessly
during the day in his lab
and drank much coffee,
his mind often flashed back to when, as a child,
he stood on the mountain
and watched the lightning strike.
Nikola also held close in his mind
an image of his young sister, Angelina,
playing near their small Belgrade home
in a rainstorm and laughing in pure bliss,

her little hands reaching
toward the down-pouring sky
with glee and abandon.

Often, on his walks
during his afternoon breaks
from his work in the lab,
he would think of this image
and smile to himself,
sometimes letting out a joyful,
quiet laugh.

Angels of Disconnect, Fast Forward

I walk along the world terrain
and see the landscape
full of the residual of Nikola's work.
Ninety-eight percent of it is of his hand.
My full lips form into a knowing, peaceful smile.

As I walk,
Thomas Edison Sr.'s two youngest progeny
walk with me in spirit—*Dot* and *Dash*,
castoffs of a new generation.
I often go to the mountain
to watch the lightning strike.
Dot and *Dash* sit with me in spirit
on the hill during the storm. It is dark.
A powerful white streak cuts
through the black of night
like nature's razor
and hits the very tree
under which I sit.
The sky's electric current
illuminates my open palms in silver light.
I look down at my hands
and think of the work they have done in the past
and what they are capable of doing in the future.
A feeling of regret mixed with hope washes over me.
I do not flinch an inch. I quietly smile and then laugh...

Each step taken leads to adaptation.
Let us hope we are going in the right direction.

Please Listen

Please listen
as I grasp for humanity
through the fragments of time,
as I reach
through the slivers of broken mirror,
this looking glass of minutes and hours
speeding by.
Please acknowledge my transmission.
Please witness I was here...
between the tethered signals
of what God hath wrought...

One hundred twelve years after the first electromagnetic
telegraph message was sent,
Tesla took his last breath.
In 1943, in room 3327 of the New York Hotel
on a cold January morning,
the monthly bill for years
paid in courtesy by Westinghouse,
a man by the name of Nikola
is found dead at the age of eighty-six.
I sit and write this verse
seventy-nine years later
cross referencing the primes
and building my logic,
hoping that there are answers
in the *n plus ones*,
that I can finally understand
the disconnect
despite our age of wireless casualties.

A Young Man Holds the Light

The body a cage, tense armor,
skin tight and heavy
like chain mail next to flesh.
From head to toe, his neurons—
fiber lightning pathways wired
to see angels in the shadows,
fired to decipher secret symbols
in mechanical structures,
seeing solutions flow through the mind's eye,
like water following gravity
to the rivers of soft-spoken tranquility.

He spends his time
by earning an hourly wage,
but he has been given the sun...
so he works in vain for money—
money that Edison will never pay him. (9)

Time passes and the light
follows his gait
in the shadows of nightly toil,
his mind inventing
where the energy and machines congeal...
to the river of nerves.
To the ocean of plasma.
To the deep anatomy
of a beating heart,
to the rhythm of alternating current.

He holds stars in parallax view,
fixed against tilted horizons,
morning askew from illuminated visions,
regretting not having dreams he can speak about.

He awakes, stumbling toward the faith in tomorrow's truths,
like a missionary trying to capture the gift of light
as if it were an inalienable right.
For this is the dove,
for he knows it to be free like God's smile.
A child plays with the light and laughs.

Through the Window

Through the window,
the world vast with possibility,
from his corner of the laboratory,
he sits, his wings clipped by the fear of people
whom he fails to know,
but whom he would give the moon.
Everything will be ordered in accordance
with the control he imposes,
and loneliness will not get in the way
despite his want for companionship.
He is here for a bigger reason,
so big that his heart might explode,
and his mind might dream of heaven,
as he sits again watching the wheels
and turning the axles to generate free energy.

Through the window, the birds will fly,
escaping his touch with such freedom,
leaving olive branches on the window sill,
letting him know of the heart of humanity still.
The buildings and factories of New York are confining,
capturing the soul of man,
but the world out there has no bounds,
and is as free as light traveling
on the white shoulders of a dove's wings.
So he will sit and make his way—a stationary navigator,
his mind drawing maps in the air,
his mind designing blueprints he will never share.

Do I know you?
There are forms of light out the window.
Do I know you?
Through the window they fly like dragons of fire—
apparitions of illumination that only I can see.

Silver Serpents of Entropy

Everything is alive.
Everything has vibrating energy.
Everything is speaking its frequency to him
in shades of motion through space and time.
As he moves from across the lab,
shuffling his belongings from here to there,
he knows it is the entropy he is fighting,
he knows it is the fire of illusion he is lighting.
But the answers always align to what corresponds in real time
to the mathematical quotients,
to the machines built of dreams and promise.

And what if I am very far away,
what if I have gone astray?
Who would know under this visage
that I am carrying an unsung message?
That I am as far away as a ship on the ocean
without a compass?

Everything is speaking its frequency,
and he tries to decipher the language,
questioning sanity in the process,
but keeping his composure,
being privy to a bird's eye view
of the Old Earth's demise,
as he quietly watches the threads of entropy
unravel like visions of wired machinery—
vibrating serpents in the air,
the silver waves of light
and shadow in his room,
his laboratory forever a tomb.

Body Resistance

By a name he cannot define,
he blocks out the feelings,
immediately upon the thought,
so that the switch turned off
impedes the action.
The wet wire of the brain
will keep it all nice and tidy in there.
And for every desire that creeps up,
he will exhale for want of nothing,
and inhale his breaths of pure oxygen,
his fists clenched in discipline,
his eyes closed and picturing
neurons firing with purpose,
his mind strapped in tight again.

He knows of the fragility
that everyone carries,
for we are ultimately one
with this planet of dirt.
By a name he cannot define,
it is all stripped bare,
the energy of the earth and grime
that makes the gears
and instruments go around.
Like the planet tilting on its axis
and spinning twenty-four/seven—
everything will fly off
if he doesn't calm down
and keep these desires to himself.
For it is just a byproduct
of the mind to justify the flesh,

and its accidental occurrence
is just a shell encasing his mind
in a cage of sinewy tissue.

The trick to alternating current
is switching directions when all is exhausted,
like a train jumping the tracks and going in reverse,
like the mind telling the body
NO to restrict the desire so it yields its power. (10)

I Get the Destination—Coffee for One

As I walk, Google Maps tells me where I am.
I look down at my phone—
I place a call and get the destination.
The signal goes through.

A voice on the other end asks,
"Hello?"
"Hi, this is just Tracy," I answer.
"Where are you?" I ask.
"I am at the coffee shop," the voice answers.
"Do you want to meet up later?" I ask,
wanting company.
"No," the voice answers in the negative. "I am working on my computer here."
"Sure," I confirm sadly. "Sounds good. Talk with you later."

I hang up. I disconnect. I look down.

Google Maps tells me where I am.
I am on 4th Street, just off of Mulberry.
I check the weather on my phone. It says rain is coming.
My phone is correct. It starts to rain.
I am without my umbrella.
I start to walk quickly to a nearby cafe.
I duck inside and order a mocha.

"Name?" the barista asks.

"It is just Tracy." I answer looking down.

She writes my name across
an empty coffee cup
and proceeds to prepare my order.

I look down.
Google Maps tells me where I am.
I look up. I am out of the rain for now.
Google Maps tells me where I am.

"Tracy!" the barista finally shouts. "Coffee for one!"

Old Earth Decay, New Earth Visions

Not more than ten years old,
I got a record player for Christmas.
The first album on vinyl I bought
was Gary Numan's *Telekon*.
By the dim light
of a small shadeless window,
night fell with the rain.
With the street lamps outside,
I curled up on my bed
and played the songs,
listening and watching
the wet cement on the streets
as the cars rumbled by,
making swooshing sounds—
Swoosh, swoosh, swoosh,
counting cars going nowhere,
being produced from the factories
to return to the factories
via junkyards and crushed metal.

It was always raining—
the windows shaking in the evening malaise,
threatening to shatter but never releasing from their sills,
attached still to the rundown houses of Detroit City,
like the eyes of my dream,
looking through the caged skull
in the sleep like state of synth music,
the soundtrack of an automated telephone operator's voice
playing from a vinyl record bought from the five and dime.

Gary Numan singing of the future,
signing off my emotions
so that I could function.
A girl in the midst of the car apocalypse,
factory chimneys blocking out the morning sun
like malevolent cathedrals,
flying buttresses
from some iron curtain nightmare
in which I made my home—
away from home—
in my head.

Normal in the Chaos

Schizophrenic episodes
like radioactive isotope lightning—
action potentials through the brain,
heightening the senses,
narrowing the pupils and widening the lenses,
so I stand on the edge of light,
riding the wave, listening, looking, paying attention to the clues—
watching and hearing everything for the record.

I will absorb the universe as the receptacle,
the instrument, the open mind
of all going on in the inter-connectivity,
of all going on in the hypersensitivity,
of all playing beyond the white noise between my ears,
despite the racing city that tells me
all is normal in the chaos.

I talk but it doesn't make sense to the doctors,
the associations not in their frame of reality,
schizophrenia not being their specialty,
so I am carted away to the fourth floor
where I have been before,
where they will tranquilize the streams
within my blood, the adrenaline slowed
so I will soon wake up from my dream,
once again, not the center of the brain cyclone,
the synchronicity speaking to me
with the most promising successful paranoia.

If I could only break on through,
I will find the answers,
I will calm the fire dancers,
I will survive the synaptic chaos
sparked by the universal embrace,
generating these episodes
that become so tiring.

"I am so tired..."

"I am so tired..."

"I am so tired..."

What Is Beneath the Disguise

It is getting harder to see Tesla's strokes
of brilliance amid the landscape,
the incorporated and patented utilities
of life's endless motion becoming tangled,
where I squint to see the beauty
in the blessed chiaroscuro corners of hotel rooms,
the skyline horizons
where the eye must focus
on the hidden shapes
and shades of glorified invention.

It is getting harder
to put all my faith in a thimble,
whisked away by time—
the small prayers and hopes,
tiny drops in the buckets overflowed
with hatred running through the streets,
like a flood of the blood, sweat, and tears,
of the millions who chase the dragon
by the tail in gigabytes
and the fiber optic lights,
oblivious to free energy's dream.

Then in the corner of my eye,
I saw him—the crouched figure of Tesla himself,
reading by the light of candles,
lit by the visitors of our chapel
who have come and gone,
thinking they have signified nothing,
yet left Nikola brilliant illumination
by which to flash a face looking back at me—
the light and shadow,

a perfect likeness, of the genius,
of all the hatred, all the sacred,
the profane and holy,
as we battle the unsung ghosts
of humanity's voices in the days and nights
of wireless solitude.

Look Back in Anger

We look back in anger,
at the past, at the present,
from the future,
and realize that progress
and our noble intent is null and void
because the equation was not balanced correctly,
but in haste and with fudged numbers
so that everyone can reap the benefits
of overpriced space junk.
Copper wire, steel, and iron.
Construction to dig up the earth
and lay down cable
despite the waves being able to travel
wireless through air
like luminous signals of instant karma.

Money makes the world go around.
They are still crawling on the surface of the Earth.
They never learned how to fly.
The circle will be broken
with our useless machinery,
making us more distant
than ever before.

The Cost of Captured Lightning

My phone and my heart have the same pulse.
Lying below the stars that shine
like nuclear flames beyond my lonely thoughts,
beyond the city's siren screams,
above the low ceilings of one-room flats,
resides all the nobodies I do not know,
who, like me,
sit in the dark
with mobile cell phones and dreams,
comforted by the electronic glow
of the Internet blurb continuum.

1882, while working for Continental Edison in Paris,
with the oil lamps still lining the streets,
Nikola worked on what Edison needed,
sending his solutions back to the States.
The magnetic induction field principle
seemed an obvious solution
to such an arduous waste of hard labor and time... (11)

... But direct current rotating generators, churning energy,
expended enormous work and danger,
sparks flying and the scent
of burning metal filling the air
with the fumes
of overworked machinery.

Magnetism and the Lonely Heart

Bless Michael Faraday in 1831,
rotating simple copper wire
in a magnetic field,
cutting across the tension of force,
until the wires obtained electric charge.
But he had not completed the thought,
the notion of magnetic fields
not going all the way,
until Nikola seized the opportunity
to present the lightning for free,
unbounded,
using the force of rotation
to his advantage
and the Earth's magnetism
as a plaything. (12)

My phone and my heart
have the same pulse,
so we are playing catch up
with the devil's horse.
North pole energy,
South pole energy,
no one is paying attention
to the wandering planet
that is our home,
so take from me the coordinates,
the compass I use to direct my soul,
and pick up your cell phones
and toss them into the ether,
to never call home again,
the world full of roaming ants
without mission control,
without a way to call out.

Edison in Kansas

Dot, can you hear me?

Dash, can you hear me?

Edison is in Kansas
and will never leave.
Edison is in the industry.
Edison is in the greed.
Edison is in the rural fields,
the stretching highways across America.
Edison is in the investments
of the good old boys' network
that wants a solid return
in inefficiency and waste.
He is languishing
in the cigar smoke-filled back rooms
of old school gentleman's clubs
where silver haired men
talk of post war profits.

Dot, what do you feel when your father tells you to get married?

Dash, what do you think when your father calls your name?

I am called to harness the light, not to own it. Tesla whispers.

I am called to harness the light, not to own it. Tesla whispers.

I am called to harness the light, not to own it. Tesla whispers.

    My hope remains alive.

A Brutal Education in America

The year was 1884
when Nikola boarded the ship S. S. *City of Richmond*
to the United States,
finding his way on foot
to Edison's New York City shop
with his letter of introduction
from Charles Batchelor.
Hired as an engineer
and promised fifty thousand dollars for his work,
he accepted the appointment
and did as he was told,
fixing Edison's mistakes and oversights.
This went on for a year without payment,
and then Nikola, the quiet servant of Menlo Park,
quit to start Tesla Electric Light and Manufacturing
in Rahway, New Jersey. (13)

Digging ditches, I abide for two dollars a day, your betrayal, your stolen means of production, I abide your deception and amorality, to displace the dirt and dig until my fingers and wrists ache with sores, but it won't be long until the hopeful will invest in my dream for I will bring the correct quotient to the people. Light always follows the path of least resistance, and I know its secrets—that it cannot be bought, only charmed by the gentlefolk who acknowledge its power.

Despite those who had backed the wrong horse,
alternating current
will override Edison's attempt
to imprison the world
and make a man rich
at the expense of keeping humanity in the dark.

My electric arc lamp is brilliant and beautiful . . . please see the perfection . . . despite the fear of the ages. I am not here to reap gain, I am here to serve Nature . . . Magic patent number 335,786 March 30, 1885. Its design is magnificent. (14)

Yet, by the end of 1886,
in the shadow
of the Union County Electric Light & Manufacturing Company
that relied heavily
in commercialization
of a utility grid and not invention,
Tesla Electric and Light dissolved,
leaving Tesla with little money
and no ownership of his patents. (15)

The War of the Currents

Do not cry little ones,
do not let your hearts be broken.
Even though you cannot separate
from the tethers
of tomorrow's imprisoned destiny,
know that your hearts
beat in unison
with the gears
of a more powerful machinery—
that of the perseverance
of innocence
in the face of the world's burden
you have inherited by default.

Your spirits carry into the future—
beyond the copper wire,
beyond the cables,
beyond the fiber optics and satellite signals,
beyond the information wars.
All the children will be waiting for you
and we shall unite
in our peace and grace
like Nature wanted all along.
So—do not cry.
Do not cry.
I walk with you
toward a better future.
You are not forgotten
despite the energy juggernauts
of ignorance.

Take my hand, Dot!

Take my hand, Dash!

Let us walk toward the light that unites us in spirit.

Let us not forget the past and present generations that walk with us.

Cutting the Cords

I've been in the cities of America,
serpentining through the streets,
unsure of my fate,
always looking over my shoulder,
but keeping my head high
and my eyes on tomorrow.

I've been in the nocturnal woods
on Canadian borders,
dreaming of aboriginal tricksters
as the Northern Lights
danced above my head,
residing in small rural counties,
the unsung heroes
haunting America's conscience
as people canoed for sport
and time stood still,
as the iron gates of shotgun shacks
swung in the silent twilight hours
of deserted miner towns,
the distant, lone train whistle
at midnight reminiscent
of rusting railway cars carrying silt
to the city to fill up
patch job potholes on sunken roads.

I've been in the theater district
of Chicago's Boystown
where the bars stayed open
until 3 am

and the actors
trickled out of their storefront theater plays
in which they dreamed of kings
and queens, and war protest,
and *The Lion in Winter*, and *Macbeth*, and *A Soldier's Story*,
the Off-Broadway repertoire and ensemble,
method acting in desperation on Friday and Saturday nights
when the avant-garde stakes were high
but the expectations were laid back and low.

I've walked over
the shifted graves of many a soul,
wandering through the cemeteries
of small towns that grew unattended
and ungroomed
into forests and waters
where wolves howled back
at the sounds of distant traffic
along the dirt roads of Route 169—
where those who perished
from past pandemics, influenza,
and black lung disease
left their visages on photographic alabaster plates
fixed to tombstones,
only to be picked off
and stolen by young vagrants
defacing history
for the sake of Halloween night souvenirs.

And all this time,
all this time,
I have witnessed the growth
of the communication between me
and the many people I have met
slowly being diminished hour by hour,
year by year as the invention grew faster,
and smaller, and cheaper,
and can now course through our veins
like the nanotechnology,
like the biophysics
of Walt Whitman's wildest dreams
in which he sang the body electric
carried by satellites
in heavenly stratospheric grace.

All this time
I have seen Nikola Tesla's light
behind the shadows of greed,
the hope of a better humanity
flicker in the storm's lightning,
knowing that the silent will be heard
when the mineral rights
and the resources have all been exhausted
and there is no choice but to cut the cords,
the wire,
and we will make
the transmission free.

Signs

The dove sits on a telephone wire,
its body white with gray wings,
perched and waiting for the sun to rise,
watching the worms
from late-night thunderstorms
wriggle onto the dry sidewalks
through wet muddy lawns,
a thin layer of frozen dew
creating rising fog in the cold morning air,
the streets beginning to stir with traffic
morphing Detroit's desolate nocturnal slumber
into dim landscapes of gray human ambition.

The street lights that once used to turn
red, green, and yellow for empty roads
start to find their purpose
as morning cars appear out of the haze,
making their way
to sluggish Monday morning destinations.
It is feeding time, and the dove swoops down
below to take her wriggling breakfast in one swallow.

The morning is beautiful in its automation.

The only things that are free are the dove's movements through time.

Flying Through the Years

Above me are the wires.
Below me are the cables.
I will see the dove again at the age of twenty.
Sped up time lapse of the years
signifying two decades
of growing pains and small epiphanies.
She is flying through my life.
Looking at me below and watching,
waiting, swooping through the tension
of the wind and the weather,
knowing full well that the Earth
pulls in a different direction
than all the human trappings of road signs,
and energy grids,
and street lights,
and street names,
and sewer grates,
and underground sanitation,
and all the old school infrastructure
with built-in obsolescence
and construction workers
forever paid for good measure.

I watch the city being built and torn down,
being built,
being torn down,
being built again.

I watch the dove
from my small window
and wait.

Know the Moment

Know that you are loved,
know that you can dream,
know that you can reach for the moon,
but also know that as the years pass,
you will see the hardness,
the need for survival
in each and every waking hour.
Know that the world is full
of those with broken hearts,
broken bodies,
broken skies,
and dark thoughts
that eclipse the soul.

Fast forward to wintry nights
in which I watched the snow fall,
blanketing the car-lined streets
in frozen white ice,
watching the animals,
the birds, stray cats, and squirrels
die in the dead of December,
disappearing
into the corners
of residential shadows
to freeze in peace,
their eyes betraying to me
as I stare
through warm interior windows
out to the night,
that they have exhausted all resources,

that they have come to the resolution
and it is to resign
to the cold mistress of silence.

I throw out bits of food in vain,
realizing it is too late,
that me and my species
have been here too long,
that we are part of the problem,
that they go starving and suffering
because we have made it so.

The rodents can balance on the wires,
they can squirrel down
into the nooks and crannies
made for cable, sewage, and power cords,
chewing at the coiled technology
and creating ghosts in the machinery
for the utility trucks and workers
punching in the clock
to uphold our decaying infrastructure.
The rodents know
through their own generational death
that they must co-exist
with this spaghetti landscape,
their survival tied
to the sloughed-off garbage
of human waste
and shed resources.

Welcome to the world,
little girl.
Fast forward,
fast forward,
fast forward,
take it in quickly
because there will be
no second chance to ask questions
of the fleeting moment in time,
for every minute asks you to be witness.
So do not ask, just know.
Know the moment for what it is.
Open your eyes and see.

Behold a Pale Horse

At the age of five,
Nikola Tesla witnessed his brother
being killed in a horse-riding accident. (16)
It shaped his life from that moment onward,
his mind often recounting the event
in photographic detail
as if the happening was etched
on celluloid film to forever serve
as a record of tragedy.
He often played the episode over and over
in his head
as if somehow the total recall
could change the outcome.

I have often seen the consequences
beyond my control.
I have seen the obsession in my own mind
to retrace the steps,
to make the chains of happenstance
alter with the willpower of the mind itself,
so that the course of tragedy
can be erased
from the causality of time.

My brother's kidneys are failing.
He has dialysis three times a week.
He gets hooked up to a machine
through a catheter in his chest
so his blood can be pumped out,
cleaned, and then pumped back in.
He sits in a chair with tubes,
valves, pressure gauges, and shiny levers.

As his blood is cleaned,
he watches a small television
with headphones for his enjoyment.
Each session takes four and a half hours.
He gets cramps while in the chair.
He gets nausea in the chair.
He gets more life in the chair.
He texts me funny emojis while in the chair . . .
Ugh! (smiley face) . . . etc.
He tries to be upbeat and positive
in the chair.

The obsession in my mind
pictures him floating in space,
tethered by a cord,
but my mind squints
and I can't see
where the umbilical cord leads.
There is no spaceship
grounding him to the Earth,
there is no station
where the fellow astronauts
are waiting with Tang
and edible sponges of protein.
In my mind's eye,
all that exists is him and the cord,
the void and black space
cradling his body in zero gravity,
going through space forever,
floating like the most brilliant human satellite.

Forty-three years
separate Tesla's brother and my own sibling.
One had twelve years of life.
The other so far fifty-four.
I turn to my brother and say,
"There is so much death, there is so much death."

He turns to me and quotes the Bible,
"And I looked, and behold a pale horse: and his name that sat on him was Death, and Hell followed with him. And power was given unto them over the fourth part of the earth, to kill with sword, and with hunger, and with death, and with the beasts of the earth." (Rev. 6:8, KJV)

With those words,
I turned to the window
and watched the snow fall.
I realized Nikola saw Death head-on
and all that would follow
in the name of human dominion.
Tesla knew full well
that he had seen Death take his brother,
and that he could never forgive himself
for being witness to the fallen.

My own brother
is floating in space,
and I cannot see where he is going.
His red river flows with the toxins.

Somehow I forgive
and let my mind let go
so I don't feel so angry at myself
for not having control.
Somehow I see Tesla
as a child
and feel his heart break.
I watch my brother
in the chair
in the films of my mind.
My brother is falling,
and there is nothing I can do
but bear witness.
There is nothing I can do
but behold the pale horse.

The War of the Currents Is Won

Nikola Tesla's simple solution
for electrical power distribution,
the rotating magnetic field principle in 1882—
the World's Colombian Exposition—Spring 1893
Chicago lit with AC beneath
a brilliant blanket of May stars,
Westinghouse at the purse strings,
Nikola at the water's edge,
tapping his foot and waiting
for the rest of the world,
to come up to speed. (17)

Beautiful Greek and Romanesque architecture,
neoclassical precision
cutting through the evening shadows,
featuring angels, and noir figures
that morph
as the Earth spins in harmony
with the celestial Gods
and Goddesses above.

Chicago, city of my youth, 1993,
one hundred years later,
I carry my briefcase,
waiting for a bus on the Miracle Mile,
wrapped in a raincoat
against the early Spring wind,
carrying an umbrella
and glancing at my watch obsessively—
I am infinitesimal
among the city of big shoulders,

buildings surrounding me
as tall as the houses of gods,
banks
and corporation headquarters
and business districts,
and speeding taxis
and rushing people
and blinking traffic lights,
and the rich
and the poor
and the young
and the old
and the desperate
and the dreaming!

I see the Chicago skyline.
I see the Colombian Exposition
a hundred years ago,
the giant statue
of The Republic
overseeing Jackson Park
and all the wandering dreamers,
all the curious investors,
all the pretty women
and close-shaven men in their suits,
following their chattering companions
in Victorian, pastel, spring-colored dresses.

City of White Light,
the industry of money
is still in your veins,

and I am racing
with the electric neon of night!
Look at my hands
and see their tan color.
A century earlier
I would have been isolated
to the Midway exhibits of the exposition
for my dark skin... (18)
Now, as the clock turns,
I witness the residue of decay
in the crumbling Chicago masonry
and flee to my freedom
like a moth to the light,
oblivious to the Icarian dangers
beneath my ambitions.

The money makes us run,
Chicago made up of the landscape
of four million hungry faces
looking toward the street lamps
of a wondrous circuitry
that never dies...

Access and the Global Brass Ring

By 1900 Nikola had envisioned it all—
global weather warning
and positioning systems,
multimedia communication—
worldwide wireless transmission
of signals, images, information,
the merge of the telegraph-telephone exchanges,
the bundled operation
of all stock tickers of the world,
ultimately the potential
to transmit wireless energy,
making it a free resource.

I tread lightly,
knowing that I walk on energy's potential
as I make my way across the Earth,
the answer beneath my feet,
the magnetic fields of the planet
holding the promise
of a magnificent power grid,
the atmosphere surrounding the globe
enveloping me in its charged power.
I walk through the resonance
of untapped miracles,
knowing fully well that Nikola
walks with me during afternoon strolls
where I let the dreams carry me away,
walking past the businesses and the banks
with their security cameras
watching over empty parking lots,
electric eyes monitoring the concrete
and ATM machines,

the drive-thru banking cubicles
and the cars carrying the faceless
on ten-minute breaks
from data entry jobs
and dead-end nine-to-fives.

The Reigns and Purse Strings

The J. P. Morgans of our cities
of engineered legacy
will tighten the reigns in
and keep a hat on
the innovation and imagination,
reaping the benefits
of the downtrodden
who pay monthly phone bills
to uphold technological crap
and dying service industries
churning to the sounds
of grid-locked supply chains
and minimum wage compensation.
Sticks and stones in the ground,
the telephone poles holding up wiring
from two hundred years ago,
crucifixes that we must finally put down,
the forces of the Old Earth and the new
co-existing so that no one looks up
or realizes the ground below
holds the key to our future
in waves of light and forces of magnetism.

So since we are not ready
to let go of the greed,
since we are not ready
to relinquish the flow of the green,
put the dreamers in little boxes,
put the inventions and intellectual property
in the archives,

let the corporations own the patents
until hell freezes over
and the satellites fall back to Earth.
So we tread lightly,
the gentlefolk
of the golden avenues of tomorrow,
always knowing that we abide
until a new day.

The Lightning in Ely, Minnesota

In 1999 I traveled from my Chicago home
to the forests of Ely, Minnesota.
A choice to leave the City of White Light
for the Northern Boundary Waters canoe area
where endless trees replace
the harsh skyline silhouettes
of skyscrapers
with the dark shadows
of oak and pine and birch wrists,
arms, and elbows reaching for the glowing,
streaming arboreal night.
I arrive by Jeep on Highway 169
in the quiet of night,
realizing at once
the absence of sirens, car horns,
and Chicago's nocturnal dialogue
leaves me beside myself
where I question who I am
in the silence of rural America.
I cannot answer the question
but know
that I have been avoiding
the answer for years.
The city has been built on hills,
some of the oldest mountains of Earth
where the moss and rocks
hide the fossils of ancient man and animal,
where I find myself listening to the wind
of aboriginal whispering spirits
of the iron range.

They call to me
and ask my purpose
in where I roam.
Again, I cannot answer.

The first sign of rain in Ely,
I witness the miracle
of the higher elevation
and greater magnetism in the atmosphere,
the strange intensity of the lightning
that strikes without the thunder following
because it silently kisses the ground and good Earth,
creating parabolas between the horizon
and the raven canopy of Milky Way ceilings.
My eyes look upward and absorb the infinite,
the haunting fear in the mind's eye
of existential wrath growing with every breath.
Then it hits me,
the epiphany of how small I really am,
traveling like an ant across the surface
of the planet like a slithering question mark
searching for a sentence,
winding this way and that,
wanting to end my journey
with a period of profundity.
Living under the guise in Chicago
like I had more purpose,
living like survival among the neon sounds of silence
meant something to the sky above,
as if surviving in the city
meant you were living the art of the deal
and had the muscle to show for it.

Then the rain starts to fall,
I hear the first drop hit
the cobblestones out my window,
yes, I am privy to the first whisper
of the storm kissing,
saying quietly so above as below,
letting me know my ears are blessed
with the sounds of nature's rituals
in the backwoods of the Canadian borders
where people have settled at the end of the road.
I listen and then suddenly,
the symphony of lights starts,
startling me from my writing desk,
so I go to the rooftop
and watch the lightning
in miraculous orchestrations.

I am humbled
by the natural wonder
of the atmosphere
displaying its nervous system
in the firing neurons of electrical energy,
the sky lighting up with the marbled veins
of electricity searching for opposite polarities
across the black forests
of our ancestral Northern coordinates.
I am beside myself
with the possibility of the future.
Nikola's dove flies
through the storms of the night,
setting my heart free.

Energy's Grail

They will label you a variable
by the cries of your generation,
they will tell you it is an X, a Y, a Z,
they will tell you
you cannot go far down a road without a sign,
they will tell you
you cannot speak for fear of not being heard,
for fear of not making
a difference shouting words to a deaf sky.

Do not swallow the medicine down
with the sweet nectar of the worker bees,
do not listen to the same words
in the headlines of yesterday's news
as if you don't have the same right to choose,
for here is your chance to wake up
and grasp the brass ring of greater things,
for here is your chance to not repeat history
with the help of the spirit of a dove's wings.

So stand up in the hunger,
stand up in the rain,
stand up and speak
for your fellow man,
stand for anything that you can name,
stand in spite of the broken backs and the wars,
and the candles behind barbed wire
that forever fuel the illuminating flame,
stand even though your legs are breaking,
stand even though your words are forsaken,

for nothing in this world is worth a damn
if you can't stand for all that is mutual
among the best in you
and the most precious grace
found in all the hearts of man.

Know that you are the same,
but know that you are Blake's tiger to be tamed,
thy fearful symmetry the best and worst in you,
if you do not fulfill the destiny
of thy brother's keeper in all you do.
So stand in your father's shoes,
despite what your father didn't know.
Stand in your mother's dress,
despite what your mother said is best.
Own the generations that you surpass
and forgive the chaos and mess.
Know that whatever they have named you
at the beginning of this journey,
is not the strength of your back
making you weak and hunched over
at the end of your quest,
making you ask of yourself,
"what do I stand for when they have come for the rest?"

Stand for anything, even if it is merely to see
beyond the bars of the window.

Look and see ... make your way and inhale.
Lightning is free and so is energy's grail.

The Heart Will Follow

"There was another and still more important reason for my late awakening. In my boyhood I suffered from a peculiar affliction due to the appearance of images, often accompanied by strong flashes of light, which marred the sight of real objects and interfered with my thoughts and action . . . They were pictures of things and scenes which I had really seen, never of those I imagined. When a word was spoken to me the image of the object it designated would present itself vividly to my vision and sometimes I was quite unable to distinguish whether what I saw was tangible or not. This caused me great discomfort and anxiety." (19)

When others think you not sane,
when the dust on the objects in the room
remind you of the decay in dawn's solitude,
the familiar and inanimate echoing
impermanence and futility in the garish light
of sunny, pointless afternoons,
when even the sacred Raven above your door
fades into patterned wallpaper,
like a caricature of black birds
repeating in cartoon madness from ceiling to floor,
showing you the comedy in obsession
over red velvet curtains in the name
of the beautiful Lenore,
you wish the mermaids
would speak your name,
giving you purpose and inspiration
from the spirits not in bottles and flasks,
but in female angels from the depths of truth
to pick up the pieces of all your broken masks.

When others think you not sane,
those unable to decipher
what the pen to paper says
like a forest lost in the trees,
when those who don't see
the value in dreams,
tell you to get some sleep,
giving you pills to kill
the illusions you keep,
when others see the frown on your brow
and attribute it to yesterday's thoughts,
yesterday's pain and the ghosts you fought,
making a mockery of your visions,
your vow to follow liberty to the ends of the Earth,
painting the roses with stripes,
you must persevere,
picking up the pen,
using the dreamer's instruments
to craft miraculous things,
never to pray and create in vain.
Know the vision is both the mind's forest
and the body of the trees,
because they will applaud
the fool only for a day,
but your dreams
will be carried
on the dragon's wings,
through the depths of hell
to the sanctuary of belief.

Nature's Light at the End of the Road

Leaving the city of neon and artificial light,
only knowing the coldness of electricity's veins
like the filament of light bulbs being controlled
by lone apartment light switches on dull eggshell walls,
only knowing the white phosphorescent tubes
glimmering above steel eatery tables
at Chicago night hawk diners and hospital halls
and surgery rooms where the white light above
is the last ethereal glow in the mind's eye
before etherized patients surrender to the unconscious
with their last hopeful prayers,
I walk in the quiet miner town with the only sounds
being my footsteps hitting dirt road and gravel,
the forest beside me a wall of endless shadow,
Nature's abyss sprawls behind and beyond
a lone standing 7-Eleven oasis
where the truck drivers on their way to Canada
stop for gas and Snickers bars,
buying more Vivarin for the road.

I walk and look up at the Ely city watertower,
wondering how the graffiti got up there,
studying the massive fish bowl atop its stem,
wondering in the dead of night
with the security lights illuminating
the tower from below,
how I never noticed a watertower in Chicago,
never took part in the quaint observations
of my advantageous solitude
now that I am alone
with the northern wolves and the red dirt.

The lakes I go to,
walking the hilly terrain,
gleam red by the early morning sunrise
because there is so much iron in the water,
not blood,
but the protein running off the rocks,
indigenous to the land itself,
and I am so small,
so small in my insecurities,
in the grasping at the straws of the universe,
taking a backpack of transcendental poetry
and metaphysics books with me
in the trunk of a Jeep
from my Chicago apartment,
hoping to get instant Karma
on my arrival to the end of the road.

All I am left with is my view
of the Milky Way
and a handful of mustard seeds
I have promised to a friend back home
to plant and watch grow
in the name of all that is Holy, Holy, Holy
and sacred on this planet
made of dirt and dead things.
More than once I come upon a pile of rocks
on the trail left by travelers
I am fortunate enough to follow
but who have not personally crossed my path.
Again I have brought books with me,
all the books I could shove in my backpack,
and so many of them are about Tesla.

Sitting on a large boulder by the water,
I smile and realize all the pictures I leaf through,
my thumb and index finger flipping
through the pages and diagrams,
are just Nikola's impressions
of the Nature now around me,
posthumous footprints of an attempt
to re-invent the great wheel we push up the hill.
Nikola guides me in keeping my eyes open
even though I am tethered to sleep.
I make my way back home in a strange terrain.
In my new home, in a small apartment,
yet again,
I lay my head down,
I dream of wireless landscapes.
Nikola is laughing.

All in good time.

"All in good time." I hear him whisper.

All in good time.

The Machinery at the Bottom of the Sea

On March 13, 1895,
Nikola's laboratory
on South Fifth Avenue in Manhattan, New York,
burned to the ground.
It had been located
on the fourth floor of the building,
and the intensity of the fire
caused the entire floor to collapse
and the building to cave in.
Many well-known people, writers, scientists, and thinkers
visited the Tesla labs of Grand Street,
33-35 South Fifth Avenue,
and 46 and 48 East Houston Street
between the years of 1889 and 1902,
however, after the fire,
Nikola chose Colorado Springs
and then Long Island
as more stable and viable
home base of operations. [20]

As I write this manuscript,
it happens to be March 13, 2022,
127 years after the fire on South Fifth Avenue.
I think of the fires
at the Alexandria Library in comparison
and regret all that we could have possibly lost
of Nikola's innovation and progress in those magical years,
the experimental evidence and notes,
and papers reduced to ash in the rubble.
I have an afterthought about Edison
and feel saddened that questions
of the fire's initial cause and destruction
to research and development go unanswered to this day.

Wireless is how I make my speech heard.
Wireless is where the signals travel in waves of light.
Wireless is where the words whisper like phantoms.
Wireless is how we dance despite the distance separating us.

The puppets are without their strings
and the machinery falls to rubble,
littering the bottom of the ocean,
creating dead zones where the green algae grow.
The John Henrys of the world are forgotten,
all their sweat and tears,
their hammers,
their nuts and bolts
of a useless utility,
absorbed into the Earth
like molten drops
from melting metal,
the blood and work
returning
to our silver steel sea
of flowing techno alchemy.

Battles with the Virtual World

Despite Nikola's battles
with his own
overactive visualization and imaginings,
he persevered,
walking the thin line
between the unreal and the very real,
the scientific.
He always had a bird's eye view
of himself as a rational,
operational human being,
despite his drifting into and out of visions.

I was once told by professionals
that I was an intelligent schizophrenic,
being able to be both in my unreal world
and the world of the rational and operational,
being very high functioning and productive.
Nikola's dove flies above me,
a manifestation of my own consciousness
looking down on the situation
and flying free and beautiful.
The white and gray creature
is able to navigate in and out
of the most precarious circumstances,
flying this way and that,
swooping down
and then rising
toward the heavens
to glide at higher altitudes.

After the Columbian Exposition of 1893,
having the encouragement and financial support
from Westinghouse and his Company,

Tesla had his dreams
of a wireless energy generator system
actualized in the ambitious construction
of the Colorado Spring tower of 1900
and the Wardenclyffe Tower
between the years of 1901 and 1902
on Long Island, in the village of Shoreham, New York.
In his mind's eye,
wireless distribution of electrical energy was possible,
establishing a long-distance power grid system
that would be uninhibited by distance and geography.
It was only a matter of building a tower
large enough to facilitate as a conductor
of the Earth's natural magnetism
aligned with the right signal engineering.

"A plant was built on Long Island with a tower 187 feet high, having a spherical terminal about sixty-eight feet in diameter. These dimensions were adequate for the transmission of virtually any amount of energy. Originally only from 200 to 300 K. W. were provided but I intended to employ later several thousand horsepower. The transmitter was to emit a wave-complex of special characteristics and I had devised a unique method of telephonic control of any amount of energy." (21)

    High hopes and miraculous visions,
    how they merge to create brilliance,
    how they leave us vulnerable before the face of God,
    bringing the tall waves close to the shore,
    then receding again into the vast ocean,
    sacred once again as part of the whole,
    our ambitions lost to history.

The Great White Elephant

After Colorado Springs burned to the ground,
Nikola went to work setting up another location
and another attempt at the project dearest to his heart—
distribution of wireless power.

"The tower was destroyed two years ago but my projects are being developed and another one, improved in some features, will be constructed." (22)

"My project was retarded by the laws of nature. The world was not prepared for it. It was too far ahead of time. But the same laws will prevail in the end and make it a triumphal success." (23)

With J. P. Morgan's money,
Wardenclyffe Tower was built,
but it was soon mortgaged
to settle Nikola's dept accrued
while staying at the Waldorf-Astoria Hotel
for years.
He believed in terrestrial resonance
that would provide the scientific capabilities
to transmit electricity
without cables or wires.
However, Marconi, by 1905
had successfully used Tesla's past research
to transmit signals across far distances,
without the use of wires
but with radio waves instead.
After years of deterioration
and lack of sustainable product,
Nikola lost ownership of Wardenclyffe in 1915.

By 1917 the tower was torn down
and the adjoining building was restructured
as a factory to produce
photographic materials by AGFA.
The AGFA factory stayed in operation
until 1992 when it finally closed. (24)

I sit here in the twenty-first century
and look around me.
Again, I see the residue
of Tesla's work in everything,
from telecommunications
to the tools of the information age and computers.
Wardenclyffe became a Great White Elephant,
a structure which once stood
for ingenious innovation
but became an albatross
as its scientific purpose eluded the inventor
who created the tower to begin with,
its use quickly becoming obsolete
with the rapid passing of time
and Tesla's lack of unification
of his concepts of terrestrial resonance
and wireless radio controlled communications.
It is not clear if he didn't understand
the final scientific solution
or if he solved the grand unified theory
of the wireless energy grid
but did not have the sustainable financial backing
to build what was ultimately necessary.

Then the fog comes in,
the cloudy, hazy recall of history
that winds its way through the landscape
and morphs the shadows into images
of the imagination and supposition.
The shadows become belief,
then fact, then collective conjecture,
turning what never was into what gets passed down
as historical document.
I see Nikola knowing this while he feeds
the pigeons and birds in the park,
knowing all too well that as he lives,
he is also witness to the lies
that will become reflections of yesterday.
Yet, he knows between the patents,
notes, reams of technical drawings and drafted ideas,
he has left the evidence for us to pick up the pieces
and move forward with the vision.
The White Elephant goes on
and the man is left to return to the dust.
What is it? I ask.
What is the solution? I beg.
Tell me through the veil
of history
despite the lies.

Keeping the Ghost Close

Why do I connect with the dead?
Why do I see the pain of Nikola's quest
in my own endeavor?
Why do I feel the anguish of his confusion?

Nikola carried the torch of an unnameable faith,
living his life not knowing what the end result would be,
or if the scribes of history would get it right
when passing down his most cherished hope.

He lived day to day, chasing phantoms of light,
only to wish that his daily whispered prayers
would somehow be heard as he retired
once again in his solitude to feed the birds.

Nikola kept the ghost close,
fearful of letting it seem so apparent,
knowing the White Elephant was his own dream
beaten down by his own desires to grasp a star,
realizing the impossibility of attaining something so far.

Nikola lost sight of the sky as the night turned to day
before he could fall to sleep and dream the desire away.
He remained forever yearning, turning like a leaf in the wind,
wrestling and twisting in his attempt at Utopia,
forgetting all that he held true
in his life's God given euphoria.

To be tethered to his vision,
was both a curse and a blessing,
for to be chained to a ghost's mission,
is to do things by any means necessary,

overriding everything he once loved
with the price of the dream as the measure of worth.

I have been in this place,
and Nikola calls my name through the ether--
he says to not dream of stars beyond your reach,
if you wish to share the dream,
if you dare to create to attain something higher,
for you will be left with the ghosts
of the pain and desire,
like a wound you try to hide from the world.

Kind Gestures

What is this life I see before me?
I put my head to the grindstone,
trying to peck at the keyboard,
my computer glowing in darkened rooms,
trying to re-create a man's motivations
with my imagination,
trying to not build incomplete puzzles
with the missing pieces,
so that I give humanity in the man its rightful due.

It is in the myriad of books and papers that time's lies are propagated,
glossing over the real delicate gesture of a man's intent,
and the electric eye of our historical writing machines,
only sees what can be truncated in the words of a headline,
as the crowd applauds what they can only see in a flash of lightning
and a bolt of glowing electricity promising spectacle.

My artificial knees and broken down legs,
have walked over Old Earth spirits,
and flown in the metal birds of New Earth planes,
These lungs have breathed the same recycled oxygen,
of the Teslas and the Edisons and the Morgans and the Westinghouses.
We all are privy to the same entropy that returns to dust.

All I can say is limited by the words I choose.
And once it is committed down to paper I lose.
So with the lens of an archaeologist in a strange land,
I try to speak delicately between the lines,
between the symbol and the story,
between the verse and allegory,
to let you know
there are Rembrandts painting in attic rooms,

there are all your dreams that go
unsung but ring forever true,
and this is why Nikola's dove flies today,
because I believe he knew the very dream
he held was fleeting as he grew old,
feeding the pigeons with a palmful of grace,
the birds catching the sustenance
of humanity's gift in mid air,
their gratitude returning threefold
in Nikola's own gestures of kindness,
as he faded into distant city horizons.

My Brother's Care

My brother had a stroke five days ago.
It was a Tuesday morning after a long night of restless sleep.
He has failing kidneys because of diabetes.
I was the one that called the EMTs.
They took him to trauma and he went through the hospital gates,
having trouble breathing, swallowing, and speaking.

He is home now and must go through rehabilitation.
Today is Saturday, the fifth day after the stroke.
He has panic attacks and can't sit down.
He cries in fear that his body doesn't do what it once did.
His brain isn't following orders.
The hand doesn't follow where the thoughts point.
The signals don't correspond to the intention.
The words don't come out the way he envisions,
just minutes before when he had the thought form.

I try to care for him the best I can.
He is under observation for the weekend.
I keep insulin and blood sugar logs
so he administers the right drugs.
He mustn't stroke out again.
He paces the living room while I keep watch.
He paces the kitchen while I keep watch.
He rocks in his chair while I keep watch.
The doctors say it will take months for the fog to lift.

I see similarities between him and Nikola.
I see Nikola's gestures not corresponding to the meanings conveyed,
people get confused by the appearance of things,
if you know what I mean?
I see similarities between my brother and you out there.

I know as you read this, it might not make sense right now,
but it is the little gestures that mean so much
in intent and our dreams.
Again, the gentle gesture of men is heard
all over the world in a slight tremble of the hand,
in a breaking of the silence with a word of meaning,
that goes into the ears with the right effect,
despite the pain it took to travel
from the brain to the vocal chords
and out into the world to reach its destination.

After Wardenclyffe

In my day visions,
Edison's children have never spoken to me.
Dot and Dash just smile as they follow me down
cobblestones where Nikola's electrified lamps glow,
along tree-lined streets bearing the names
of dead benefactors who built the city
with their money and power.
Even on Edison Boulevard,
the paths are illuminated with alternating current
and Tesla's glowing arcs of light.

Beautiful, beautiful cities of light,
Nikola's dove flies high over
the business district tonight,
as Wall Street insomniacs count money.
The dogs will fight for dominion
in the stock and trade communion—
the Edisons of tomorrow stealing
the next great idea,
bogarted in good faith.

After Wardenclyffe,
Nikola Tesla sees in the corner of his eye,
what I see every day.
Dot and Dash young and free,
bending down to cup the elixir
of a silver stream with little hands
to drink from the river of the eternal life,
of man's spirit in light of invention
where the machines whisper in the dark,
shining electric eyes to ignite the spark.

My brother and I
hold the torch,
passing it down,
knowing full well,
with all the wires of communication,
with all the global signals flying North,
by default
humanity's love cannot be spoken
in words.

Nervous Breakdowns

Tesla in 1906 turned fifty years old,
having his shop eventually re-opened at 165 Broadway, Manhattan,
with no real capital or money from patents,
he stayed in hotel rooms,
like the Waldorf-Astoria and the St. Regis,
inventing the bladeless turbine and serpentining through
financial hoops
of both debt and lack of rent payment for either his residence
or his labs. (25)

The man didn't require much space,
usually single rooms with double beds,
on occasion ordering room and cleaning service,
he'd entertain at his labs instead of having guests in his
private chambers.
His habit of letting the birds
into the hotel rooms through open windows
made a mess of the floors, walls, and furniture.

Despite the avian dirt and grime,
he still feared the most germs from another living soul,
wearing gloves whenever the chance
afforded to keep his hands clean. (26)
Yet, Heaven forbid he have
an offending meal placed across his plate.
Heaven forbid those who are fat, shabby, crude,
or who resemble the Falstaffs of the world cross his path,
jarring his sense of sublime perfection
in the human form and character.
Heaven forbid, Nikola, with the birds speaking only to him,
be thought of as ordinary.

Heaven help him, Nikola believed
in the American individualism of the twentieth-century promise.
But it was his own bouts with paranoia
and OCD that impeded him the most,
so much so that his comprehension suffered
and his problem solving in inventing was compromised.
The puzzle could never be put back together again,
the phantoms of delusion hovering
over the once hopeful and driven inventor,
like clouds in an expansive unforgiving sky,
his mind seeking the face of God in the motion of birds.

We Are Not Who We Seem to Be

I see the waitress bring in the plates.
I see the waiters as they wait.
I see the store clerks scanning items,
I see them as they bag my purchases.
I see the street sweepers being driven.
I see the homeless sleepers by the river.
I see all the roles we play just to get paid
so we may survive yet another day.
But do I understand the sacrifice,
do I grasp the meaning behind the action?
Have I overlooked the story that has been
written, printed, and booked like so much ink
bled off the pen to be put in place of the thing?
I remember selectively, I forget conveniently.
I write words down as a note to myself,
a message in a bottle to let me know,
I have been where I have been before.
And I have nothing to speak of as legacy,
except the power of witness in my life,
the experience I share as the miracle,
of our small and impermanent footprint,
across the transparent waters of time,
that flow forward with those mortal regrets,
washing away all the faces
in the past that we forget.

Don't Mind the Clock

I know of a poet who died of a broken heart.
Each time she would sit before the machine,
she would hear the clock ticking,
distracting her from the task at hand.
Typing tests are always slower,
when they are timed with a stop watch.
The body falls forward,
and you take in less and give more.
The body leans seaward,
for it is the ocean that promises the shore.
The body motions toward entropy,
but then I digress, I digress
and the mind follows with the logic that is best.
So do not weep for the poets
who die of broken hearts.
They will indeed survive,
in the lightning,
the clouds,
the planet's spherical quest.
Weep for those who barricade,
and steal, and confiscate, and repossess.
Weep for those who seek profit in need
when the bird is caged within the chest.
This is the test.
This is the test—
remembering the history
of the dreaming quest,
despite all that has been taken
in ignorance.

Long Day's Journey into Light

In 1909, Marconi won the Nobel Prize for
his U.S. Radio patents, yet Tesla sued for
ownership of the intellectual property.
It wasn't resolved until after Tesla's death in 1943,
when the U.S. Supreme Court upheld Nikola's radio patent,
apparently as a maneuver to avoid a lawsuit with Marconi
over the use of his patents during World War I.
The government wanted to avoid a payout and settled
Tesla's suit to get out of retributions and damages.

In 1915 Tesla was also passed up for the
Nobel Prize
along with Thomas Edison because of the
controversy of their rivalry.
In 1917 he won the Edison Medal
for his early work with polyphase
and high-frequency
electric currents.
In 1919 Tesla writes his autobiography
for the
magazine "The Electrical Experimenter."

Nikola continues to invent
past the age of fifty
despite his work being
stolen, pirated,
and falsely appropriated
for corporate gain.

He remains a nomad,
his hotel bills mounting,
and his company dwindling.
the hotel cleaning services.
By 1934 Westinghouse pays
his residency bills,
$125 dollars a month,
so he can reside
at the New Yorker Hotel, Room 3327,
until his passing.

In 1937 Nikola is struck by a taxi
on his way home.
He refuses doctor's care
and finally dies from health complications
on January 7, 1943. (27)

The Oath of the Gentlefolk

A photon can sometimes be a wave.
A photon can sometimes be a particle.
It always takes the path of least resistance
and gets where it has to go.
The messenger boys will be paid,
for their muscle, brawn, and devotion,
no matter what the mission.
This is why they are expendable after the signal is received.
A dime a dozen, wearing suits and shiny shoes
for bureaucratic efficiency and societal safety,
convinced what they are doing is for the protection,
of the better interests involved in investment.

The nature of light can be liquid,
if the vessel calls for it.
The nature of light can be quick,
if the flame captures the shadow's evil spirit.
The nature of light always prevails,
because it knows good and peace,
following through to where
it is needed the most
to illuminate the shapes of monsters,
and to shed light on the prison bars,
of those put away for what's in their heads.

You elude me, dear Nikola.
You left your legacy to all,
but so few realize the gift.
I am here, faced with
conversations about the weather.
What can one talk about, but the weather?
What can one realize, but hope is a thing with feathers?

Should I turn a cold shoulder and feed pigeons in the park?
Again, light always takes the path of least resistance,
for by the code of the gentlefolk,
light must illuminate the dark.

Hope Is Watching the Weather

I sit on the porch in the rain and watch the lightning overhead.
There is no telling where the wind will blow.
Like an aboriginal sky watcher,
I listen to the sounds of the coming storm.
The sun has set on a century of invention.
The twenty-first century is upon us.
My brother and I carry the torch.
You are miles away but our signals travel at fiber optic speed.
It takes seconds to flip a switch
with accurate results.
The voices coming through are only delayed
when the satellites get interference from a tilting planet.

Today, I sit on a porch in Minnesota and watch the lightning dance.
Dot and Dash are with me, each sitting on either side of me.
We three, trinity of thee,
progeny of what could possibly be.
Watching the energy of light that is one in the same,
playing in form and function within our realm,
on this small planet that we can barely name.

"I anticipate that many, unprepared for these results, which, through long familiarity, appear to me simple and obvious, will consider them still far from practical application . . . a mass which resists the force at first, once set in movement, adds to the energy. The scientific man does not aim at an immediate result. He does not expect that his advanced ideas will be readily taken up. His work is like that of the planter—for the future. His duty is to lay the foundation for those who are to come, and point the way. He lives and labors and hopes with the poet who says:

Schaff', das Tagwerk meiner Hande,
Hohes Gluck, dass ich's vollende!
Lass, o lass mich nicht ermatten!
Nein, es sind nicht leere Traume:
Jetzt nur Stangen, diese Baume
Geben einst noch Frucht und Schatten." (28)

Daily work—my hands' employment,
To complete is pure enjoyment!
Let, oh, let me never falter!
No! there is no empty dreaming:
Lo! these trees, but bare poles seeming,
Yet will yield both fruit and shelter! (Goethe's "Hope.")

Nikola's Dove

If you stand incredibly still,
and reach your palms outward,
with closed eyes and still breath,
you can feel the Earth turning ever so slightly
on its axis, pointing you forever North.

There are offerings before you.
There are those who have paved the way.
Nikola's dove flies over the graves
beneath the oceans of our sunken dreams.
She kisses the sky with silver tipped wings,
looking down at the grid made by watchmen
who wound the clocks tight and accurate,
so the world would not break from the weight of it.

Witness her on her journey,
and pay no mind to the lies,
pay no mind to the misinterpretation,
of every calculation that ties
you to the bean counters and deal makers,
those who call you brethren
but bring nothing but the setting sun.

Go and innovate in flight
for the quest is yours.
I hold Dot and Dash's hand
and watch the lightning strike.

Go and fly with her, breaking the night,
until the horizon promises the communion
of the eternal dream.

Remember, it is your right
to fly like the creatures above.
It is your right
to follow Nikola's dove
toward our city of golden light.

Notes

1. Thomas Streissguth, *Communications: Sending the Message* (Minneapolis, Minnesota, 1997), 36.
2. Ibid, 37.
3. Ibid, 5–61.
4. "The Edison Family: Thomas A. Edison," *Edison Innovation Foundation* (https://www.thomasedison.org/the-edison-family).
5. Samuel F. B. Morse Papers at the Library of Congress: 1793 to 1919 (https://www.loc.gov/collections/samuel-morse-papers/articles-and-essays/invention-of-the-telegraph).
6. "The Edison Family."
7. Edward Marshall, "No Immortality of the Soul," *The New York Times*, October 2, 1910 (https://www.nytimes.com/1910/10/02/archives/-no-immortality-of-the-soul-says-thomas-a-edison-in-fact-he-doesnt-.html).
8. Nikola Tesla, *My Inventions and Other Writings* (New York: Penguin Group, 2011), vii, Introduction by Samantha Hunt.
9. "Nikola Tesla Quits Working for Edison," *World History Project* (https://worldhistoryproject.org/1885/nikola-tesla-quits-working-for-edison).
10. Nikola Tesla, "A New System for Alternating Current Motors and Transformers," delivered before the American Institute of Electrical Engineers, May 1888 (http://www.tfcbooks.com/tesla/1888-05-16.htm).
11. Ariel Roguin, Nikola Tesla: The Man Behind the Magnetic Field Unit, Journal of Magnetic Resonance Imaging, February 24, 2004 (https://doi.org/10.1002/jmri.20002).
12. Nikola Tesla, *My Inventions and Other Writings*, 64–79.
13. "Nikola Tesla Forms Tesla Electric Light and Manufacturing Company," *World History Project* (https://worldhistoryproject.org/1886/nikola-tesla-forms-tesla-electric-light-and-manufacturing-company/).

14. "Tesla's Arc Light Technology," *Lab-Tesla* (https://www.lab-tesla.org/arc-lights.html).

15. "Tesla Electric Light and Manufacturing," *Tesla Science Center* (https://teslasciencecenter.org/pivotalmoments/electric-light-company/).

16. Nikola Tesla, *My Inventions and Other Writings*, 5–6.

17. Margaret Cheney, Robert Uth, and Jim Glenn. *Tesla – Master of Lightning* (MetroBooks/Barnes and Noble, 2001), 22–34.

18. World's Columbian Expositio (https://en.wikipedia.org/wiki/World%27s_Columbian_Exposition).

19. Nikola Tesla, *My Inventions and Other Writings*, 9.

20. David J. Kent, *Tesla: The Wizard of Electricity* (Fall River Press, 2013), 131–160.

21. Nikola Tesla, *My Inventions and Other Writings*, 64.

22. Ibid.

23. Ibid, 65.

24. "Contruction Begins on Tesla's Wardenclyffe Tower," *World History Project* (https://worldhistoryproject.org/1901/construction-begins-on-teslas-wardenclyffe-tower/).

25. "Nikola Tesla," *Wikipedia Free Encyclopedia* (https://en.wikipedia.org/wiki/Nikola_Tesla).

26. Gilbert King, "The Rise and Fall of Nikola Tesla and His Tower," *Smithsonian Magazine,* February 4, 2013 (https://www.smithsonianmag.com/history/the-rise-and-fall-of-nikola-tesla-and-his-tower-11074324/).

27. "Nikola Tesla," *Wikipedia Free Encyclopedia* (https://en.wikipedia.org/wiki/Nikola_Tesla).

28. Nikola Tesla, *My Inventions and Other Writings*, 167.

About the Author

TRACY ROSS is a poet and writer from Minnesota. She is a recipient of grants from the Minnesota State Arts Board and the Prairie Lakes Regional Arts Council (McKnight Foundation). *When Lightning Strikes (Nikola's Dove)* is her newest work of poetry. She is the author of *Binary Logic*, a collection of short stories (Liminal Books, 2022), and is currently working on a collection of essays on popular culture. She teaches undergraduate writing and research and is an MFA (poetry) graduate of Augsburg University in Minneapolis. You may learn more about her and her work at https://www.rosspoet.org.

Shanti Arts

Nature • Art • Spirit

Please visit us online
to browse our entire book catalog,
including poetry collections and fiction,
books on travel, nature, healing, art,
photography, and more.

Also take a look at our highly regarded art
and literary journal, *Still Point Arts Quarterly*,
which may be downloaded for free.

www.shantiarts.com

www.ingramcontent.com/pod-product-compliance
Lightning Source LLC
LaVergne TN
LVHW020936090426
835512LV00020B/3385